Words I've Failed to Say

Tatiana Gonzalez

BookLeaf
Publishing

Presentation by *BookLeaf Publishing*

Web: www.bookleafpub.com

E-mail: info@bookleafpub.com

ISBN: 9789357442909

First edition 2023

What Have I Become?

The mirror stares straight back at me
I'm looking hard but I don't recognize a single
thing I see
The girl in the mirror looks unhappy,
Dull,
Tired,
Hopeless.
I can't seem to find the person I once was,
Before this disease,
or illness,
 or whatever you want to call it
Took hold of me and everything I once was.
Don't be fooled, just because you can't see this
illness,
doesn't mean it isn't deadly.
It can breed in the back of your mind and lay
festering for years,
waiting for the perfect moment to strike,
when you feel the most alone and empty,
before it finally decides that the control you had
over your life
And your body
 was more important than the late night drives
and milkshakes with your friends
Or sharing a sundae with your significant other.

When it decided that birthday cake wasn't
acceptable
And watermelon with whipped cream was the
only way you could go
It drains you of every last bit of life you once
had in you
 until your sat in your room, alone
On a saturday night,
Because it pushed your friends and family away
And now the only thing you gained from it
caused you to lose not just everyone around you,
but yourself as well.

Control

Everyone else hated you
and what you represented
Your reactions and need for control
The sharp words that would cut others
as they were thrown their way

But,
I miss you
and people hate that too
You made me finally feel put together
I miss the control

The cold, shaky hands
The dark circles and sunken face
that could rival something
straight out of a Tim Burton film
The pale, deadly glow
that had shown through on my skin

The structure I have so desperately craved
all my life
And finally having the façade of that
felt like I had, at once, gotten that
breath of fresh air
I had been so desperately grasping for

Lost

You were both important to me in ways that I
couldn't comprehend at my age
You took care of me when my parents weren't
home
And even though you were my great
grandparents
It, at times, felt like you were my parents from
the beginning.
All the memories,
Libraries we visited
Horse races we went to where you'd always pick
the pink number 8 for me and the yellow number
4 for my little brother.
The hot chocolates and cooking shows we would
watch
All have a place in me that won't ever be erased.

I was eight years old when we got the call.
I'll never forget the strangely warm November
day,
 it felt like part of my soul had been ripped from
me.
I didn't understand grief and what it meant
I just knew there were these strange and
unfamiliar feelings

Swirling throughout my body.
I began to fear them because of the thought of
them swallowing me whole one day.
After your wake, I swore to myself
Whether I realized it or not, that I could not face
what I felt
I would rather bury them deep within and hope
That one day I don't burst at the seams because
of them.

Nine years later and now I'm seventeen
It was the last day of my junior year when I
woke to a call from my grandmother
It was a call I knew I'd get at some point
I just wish it hadn't been so soon
There wasn't enough time
But this time it wasn't the same reaction as last.
Deep down I've always known
I lost both of you at once.

You Should Have Been There

When I was younger, I had always imagined you both
sitting front row at my wedding
As I said my vows with a grin on my face
But, as I aged, I knew that maybe
that dream was not so possible
So, I settled for you both at
my High School graduation
But, as fate would have it
that was not as plausible as I once imagined

He left when I was eight
I graduated ten years too late
She left last year
If only she could have held on
twelve more months

You both should have been there

Empty

I try to fill this
ever-growing void
Just when it seems
as if it is finally satisfied,
it wraps its arms around me
and engulfs me
in its dark, cold,
but comforting, embrace

Waves

The waves washed away from the shore
And during those few quiet moments
I finally felt at peace
Just for me to be swarmed once more
By the waves that always engulf me
tugging me down
as night falls
And at times, I am caught by surprise
While the sun still shines
Once more, it washes over me
The feelings of grief,
Of loneliness and longing

Just Three Words

Those three words
rolling off the tip of my tongue
ever so delicately
and rather easily.
They were once so foreign to speak
as if it was a phrase from an unknown language.

Now, those three simple words
coat the inside of my mouth
with a warmth I could never
begin to fathom

Home

I never knew that one day
I would be staring into those brown eyes
and feel more at home
than I ever have in any house
And suddenly, all I need to feel at peace
is with your arms wrapped around me
Your warmth engulfs me
whenever it is most needed

And that's when I knew the love I have for you
could not compare to any other

Three Wishes

If a genie ever granted my three wishes,
The first would be
to wake up every morning
with you beside me
As the sun's rays peak through the curtains
and dance across your soft, golden skin

The second would be
to always make you smile
Because there is something so sweet
and comforting
seeing that grin spread across your face
and your eyes crinkling

And my third would be
To have the chance to spend
the rest of my days and nights
with you
Because all I really need
to feel at peace
is you

I Want You

I want you when it's two in the afternoon
and we are laughing
while we eat our ice cream,
talking about our memories
from years long ago
and where what we have now,
was only ever
in my wildest imagination

I want you when it's two in the morning
and everything feels dark
When that little voice in your head
begins to raise its voice
until its screaming at you
Trying to find validity in your insecurities
I want to be there
to hold you and try my hardest
to help quiet those thoughts
and push them out to bay

One Too Many

That's how it always ends
I say I'll have just one or two
Next thing you know
the bottle is glued to my hand
and half is gone
already infecting my bloodstream
It's as if it is suddenly my only lifeline
It makes everything else seem so insignificant
Which can feel addictive
Especially for someone who has always
lived and been stuck in their head
The venom poured from those
deadly bottles
filled with medication to silence,
for a moment,
all the unwanted thoughts that constantly
swarm my brain
from morning to night
And so then,
I realize its the next morning
And yet again, I've had
One too many

Tired

Lately, I'm so tired
Getting out of bed was beginning
to feel like second nature
once again
But, now as I lay with open eyes
I dread the second my feet
will hit the cold wooden floor
As this empty hole and
unbearable weight
fight for me
to stay at rest

I fight back knowing
I can't succumb to these voices
So, I get out of bed

But don't be fooled,
that same empty hole and weight
have still found their way
to travel along with me
And claw their way into
the dark cracks in my brain
As I struggle to maintain these
boring, mundane tasks

My Muse

What happens when your muse,
is no longer your muse?
They don't spark the creative flow
like they once had
not long ago
Instead, you're filled with thoughts
and feelings of monotony
Conversations with them
seem as if you're only
conversing with a brick wall
Or, does this just mean
My muse is still my muse
but rather made me, for once,
feel comforted by the mundane

Pipe Dream

I've always loved literature
Reading, writing,
you name it
And in another life
I think I could have done it
Maybe I would have been gifted
with an extraordinary talent
that made expressing these
extensive and complex emotions
more delicate and graceful
Or rather more raw and unrefined

But I wasn't
And so, I will have to settle
with that thought
being just another
silly little
pipe dream

Burning

I feel everyone's eyes on me
burning through the back of my skull
like an ant,
being burned by the light
reflected through a magnifying glass
The thoughts in my head are too loud
to drown out
Each bite I take makes me sink
closer and closer to the floor
And every nerve in my body is telling me
to let it escape
But I can't
I need to keep it down,
Bottle every thought and emotion I feel
If I don't, I won't let only myself down
but everyone else as well

Nostalgic

I am nostalgic
nostalgic for a time
where I was turning into something
I was never meant to be
My attitude was sharper
than the blades I had pressed into my legs
not long after I was meant to be healing
from the same sickness
that poisoned my brain
with irrational and ravenous thoughts
The voice being ever so critical
You would think it was a reincarnation
of some higher power

I'm nostalgic for my purple, ice hands
never finding a proper source of hear
to keep the blood flow circulating
and when the room would blacken
as I would find myself standing

Winter

The winter of my life lasted two years
rather than three months
as nature would have it
And at moments,
it seemed as if I could see spring begin
to peak through
the storms and the cold
just for it to be covered up once more
And so, I sat waiting around
for the next storm to pass
in hopes that maybe spring
had finally come
once and for all

little bubbles

I stand here
blood bubbling at the open seams
no one else is here
no one else can hear me
they don't hear the violent sobs
as I sit in the car
they don't hear the thoughts running through my
head
like wild little roaches
infesting my rotting brain
the same brain that wishes my body
would just catch up to where my head is already
half-dead
that same brain that toasts whenever
those small, little bubbles appear

Soulmate

what's a soulmate?
is it someone who listens
to every word you say
like its the first time you've met?
someone who knows you're go-to order
at the café downtown?
or someone who brings you flowers every week?

well, truthfully
I don't know
no one does

but maybe its the person
you call first to tell important news
or who sits with when those thoughts
are just a little too loud
or the person who would make
you hot cocoa when you are sad

Pressure

I sat as I firmly gripped
my phone
holding my breath
waiting
for the camel's back to break
because there were just one too many straws on
it
but it didn't
and that was worse
because now there's a choking sensation
like the weight, I put on myself
is finally crushing me
and forcing all the air
out of my lungs
and I can't help but feel as if nothing
or no one could prevent it
from fully crumbling

mirror

I look straight ahead
an unfamiliar face
staring directly back at me
I don't know who she is
or what exactly she wants
but I can tell she feels unwelcome by me

she seems to think
we actually know each other
like we have lived the same life

but I haven't seen a girl like this ever
her sweetness seems so naive
her love of the arts being gauche
and inauthentic
her sparkle shining so bright

I could have never been her
I could never be her